The Places We Empty

The Places We Empty

Poems by

Julie Weiss

Cover design by Shay Culligan

ISBN: 978-1-954353-83-1

Kelsay Books
502 South 1040 East, A-119
American Fork, Utah, 84003

For my parents, Nancy and Gerry

Trigger Warning

Many of the poems in this book contain graphic depictions of miscarriage, rape, murder, debilitating illness, racism, homophobia, suicide, and torture.

Acknowledgments

I would like to express my gratitude to the following journals where many of these poems first appeared, sometimes in earlier versions or with different titles:

Alexandria Quarterly: "Imagine"

Anti-Heroin Chic: "Silence"

Glass: A Journal of Poetry (Poets Resist): "What She Remembers"

Indolent Books (What Rough Beast): "Coronaversary, April 12th, 2020"

Kissing Dynamite Poetry: "This Morning"

Perhappened: "Serendipity: A Golden Shovel"

Poetry Quarterly: "Not Ready"

Praxis Magazine: "Ice Rink," "Funeral Toll," "Again"

Random Sample Review: "California on Fire"

Sky Island Journal: "Poem of My Life," "Seagull," "Wish"

Songs of Eretz Poetry Review: "Messenger"

Stonecoast Review: "Fly"

The American Journal of Poetry: "The Bicycle"

The Beautiful Cadaver Project Pittsburgh: Is it Hot in Here or Is It Just Me? Women Over 40 Write on Aging: "Thanatophobia"

The Broken Spine Artist Collective: "On Our Way to School"

The Magnolia Review: "The Reasons I Won't Be Coming," "The Places We Empty" (previously titled "Silence")

The Meadow: "What I Left Behind"

Trampset: "Left Behind"

Writers Resist: "Ruled Suicide" (previously titled "Lynched")

Thank You

So many wonderful people had a hand in making this book. Firstly, I'm bursting with love and gratitude for my family and friends, who have long believed in me and my poetry. My mother read many of these poems with fervor and delight before they were published, my father always insisted I would realize my childhood dream, even when I didn't believe it myself, and my brother, Jeff, has been cheering me on from across the pond since I started this journey. Mil gracias to my beautiful wife, Olga, for loving a woman whose head is always in the clouds of a poem. If you weren't there to ground me, I'd surely float away. To my equally beautiful children, Ariana and Gabriel: I'm thankful for your laughter, wit, and gentle hearts. My love for all of you is a universe. Thank you to Karen Poppy for inspiring me, through your own sensational comeback, to return to writing after so many years. I am forever indebted to my late university professor and mentor, Virginia De Araujo, to whom "Fly" is dedicated. If it hadn't been for your passion, love, and honesty, I wouldn't be the poet I am today. Virginia, I carry you in my heart and words, always. My deepest gratitude goes out to fellow poets Gloria Collins and Kirsty MacKay for your friendship, attention to detail, ear for music, and above all, your love and support, stretching back over twenty years. I'm eternally grateful to Kate Evans, Megan Merchant, and Persis Karim for setting aside some of your precious time to pen such exquisite and insightful blurbs. A special mention of gratitude goes to the extraordinary artist Danelle Rivas, who allowed me to use her painting for the cover. Thank you to Marc Alan Di Martino, who urged me to send my manuscript to Kelsay Books, and to Karen Kelsay for the thrilling acceptance. And last but certainly not least, I'm thankful to Writers United members Marc Alan Di Martino, Betsy Mars, Kirsty MacKay, Anita Haas, Andrea Maurice, Valerie Frost, and Anannya Uberoi for your friendship, encouragement, enthusiasm, and shared passion for the written word. I'd be on my own out here, digging poems out of a literary vacuum, if it weren't for all of you.

Contents

*If you observe attentively
you will even find wisdom in shadows.*
—African Proverb

California on Fire

She can't read the words through the smoke,
  can't decipher the letters on the blackened sign

so she keeps walking, in whatever direction
  feels the coldest. What good are words anyway

when flames are rising out of the earth,
  fanning their wings behind her, across

the night sky, as if a thousand snarling demons
  have been unleashed from the underworld.

What good are words when her lover's body
  lies crushed under fallen planks,

when their faithful old hound has vanished,
  when all the memories they made together

have been drained of color, have ruptured and lie
  under charred wood. The old space between

the walls of her home seems so splendid
  in retrospect, so plentiful of life, so dazzlingly hers

that she cannot reconcile herself to the monotony
  of debris, indistinguishable as a pile of bones,

slight enough to walk over, had her feet not been bare,
  had she lingered until the embers cooled.

There were people who turned back, keen to retrieve
  any relic of their former life that may have surfaced

in the aftermath, but what good are keepsakes
       when the baby cradled in her arms has stopped breathing?

She has found a shelter where they give her
       fresh clothes, a bowl of soup, a mattress

in the corner. She suspects they are skirting
       protocol when they pretend her daughter isn't

dead, isn't really nursing under the shawl
       and though words have burned up in her throat,

crumbled to ashes on her lips, she is grateful.
       Someone has mounted a television on the wall:

she sees that man surveying the destruction,
       his face on fire, whether from sun or oil or plain

hate she couldn't say, but he is contorting his words,
       he is blaming her state, blaming her for not raking

forest leaves, blaming them all, as if they had
       contrived the demise of their own families.

The Bicycle

There it lay, red and glistening, abandoned
in the middle of the plaza, flipped
sideways as if in a fit of rage or despair,

wheels spinning madly under the wind's
nimble fingers. The bicycle belonged
to a child, but there were no children

prancing about, no pounding feet,
no shrieks of glee, just her
passing through on a stormy

Sunday morning, the click of her heels
echoing, leaving exclamation points in her wake,
ricocheting off fountains and statues,

off benches where people normally sat,
kissing or conversing, where women stopped
to rest, hands cradling their round bellies.

Her umbrella, too, lay abandoned
back there, sprawled across her bathroom
floor, like a child in the thick

of a temper tantrum. After the ache,
the blood, after she knew he had left
her body and curled up into the universe

she had craved the rain, the howl of thunder,
the chill that would shiver her bones apart.
She had wanted to soak her memory to a blur.

The bicycle was wet to the touch, slippery
as vernix, cold as a corpse. When she was sure
no one was looking, she picked it up, took it home.

What She Remembers

Most of all, she remembers red: the color
of her lips pressed around his penis,
not shimmery red, like the smudge of lipstick
left on the cocktail glass he had offered her
but rivulets of blood his teeth had loosened
when he bit into them and whipped it out.

By then, his boy-next-door smile had mutated
into some beast even a mother could abhor,
his grasp on her shoulder had hardened,
the blood vessels in his eyes had multiplied,
had grown arms and were strangling her.
Downstairs, the music and merrymaking kept on.

She can't remember how her dress ended up
around her ankles, slashed in places
as if by knife or claw, or at what point
he had wedged cherries into her vagina
like a bad joke. When a friend took her home
the next morning, her insides burned, so she presumed
he had wedged his penis in there, as well.

She does remember a click—the door locking
from the outside, a bed with gaudy red sheets,
ropes and handcuffs and what looked like
assorted mechanisms of torture that set her voice
aflame. She isn't religious, but she remembers
the omnipresence of his hand, muffling her screams.

Even now, he's everywhere in this office, flapping
his red-stained wings like a Stymphalian bird,
screeching obscenities into her ear
as she tells the director what she remembers,
as he looks at her with disdain, with disbelief,
with a sizeable check in his pocket, recently donated
to the college by the fine young man's family.

Silence

They stuffed dirt in her mouth so she wouldn't talk
but they needn't have worried. Afterwards, she lost

all her words, as if they had tumbled out of her mind
in a moment of distraction, like loose coins falling

out of a pocket, or petals spiraling toward the earth.
Even before she reached home, she had pulled a veil

of silence over her face, her features so blank, so gray,
at dinner her parents wondered what storm had passed

through her. They didn't pry, presumed their daughter
was entangled in a teenage love saga,

figured she'd find a way to loosen the knot.
In a sense, they were right. Love had set the events

in motion: the note, intended for the girl two desks over,
intercepted. The ambush at the creek. The blindfold

superfluous since it didn't obscure their voices.
The slurs as they held her down, raped her one by one.

It was their duty, they said, to right a sexual wrong.
How could she ever fish those words out of the water,

stuff them in her backpack, bring them home
to cook? Instead, she mastered the art of body language.

A shrug could mean *I don't know* or *I don't care.*
A nod conveyed compliance, desire, or when her memories

short-circuited and her mind flickered off, pleasure.
A head shake translated to a thousand variations of *no*.

By summer she had found solace in music, the heavier the better,
the kind that cracked wall paint, knocked plates off shelves,

thundered the voices out of her head. She made no apologies
for bellowing lyrics as raw as the ache they had left between

her legs. What did it matter that the psychiatrist devised
a fancy interpretation of the slashes on her wrists?

It irked her, the way he scrawled *a denial*
of self-inflicted wounds in the space below her name,

a mere fragment bereft of a subject, a figure floating around
without a head. She would have told him so before sprinting

out of his office, but her words were still snagged on shrubs,
twisted around vines, buried in soil. That's where they found

her, an empty bottle of sleeping pills near her hand and a letter
in her pocket that began: *once upon a time, I loved a girl.*

Ruled Suicide

—for Robert Fuller

There's a body hanging from a branch
        outside City Hall and nobody is talking.

        The sky cowers under its predawn cloak.
The tree holds its breath.

This is not a Discovery Channel documentary
        set in the Antebellum South

        or an antique postcard from the 1920s
sold as a souvenir to grinning spectators.

Did they jostle each other for a spot
        at the front, inches from the man

        being hoisted to his death?
There's a body hanging from a branch

in a 21st century California suburb.
        The tree is full, leaves glistening,

        much like the one we lean against
while picnicking with our children,

white and unafraid, oblivious
        to the nooses that have squeezed

        the breath out of Black families
for centuries.

Whoever claimed time marches onwards
        lied. Decades struck backwards

under the lash of the past
as the morning newscast fades

to black and white.
        Suicide, they'll say. A coincidence:

        all these unbalanced, pandemic-stricken
Black men hanging themselves

in the thick of a revolution.
        Now slumped on the ground, his body

        blazes in the colors of sunrise
and nobody is talking.

Lost

Rains fall hard as rocks
yet she manipulates the path with her cane,
slipping over the cobblestones on her way to the park,

third time today, the ritual, which for years belied
the cracks in her bones, the steady creaking,
now drained of significance. She has no time to weep.

This morning, the house was silent, shocking as spirits,
no weak bark to wake her at eight, no wet tongue
or claws clattering across the hardwood floor.

Just in case, she filled the small plastic bowl
with chicken and rice, the large one with spring water,
placed the squeaky alligator on the blanket, next to the ball.

At the park, she rustles bushes, rummages through trash cans,
peers into the faces of all the dogs who run up to her
snatching biscuits and sausages from her outstretched hand.

When the sky turns dark and everyone has gone home,
the only thing left in the muddy grass
is his name, scattered about like raindrops.

On her way back, she walks past the lake, breaks
the murky surface with a coin, certain the rascal
will come home tomorrow. She walks, oblivious

to the animal bobbing among discarded junk and
to the distant laughter of neighborhood children
who had made a game of dog underwater.

Not Ready

She adjusts her pillow, glances around the room:
television, lamp, explosions of white everywhere.
Eyes drowned in silence, body parts strung
with wires and tubes, she is more fossil than flesh.
But she is not ready yet, there is so much to do.

She watches a spider in the corner weave its bed
out of rainbow silk. It leaves her a pattern of stories,
each strand a passage, and she reads her life
turning sheer, dusty pages. It drops into a pot
of tulips, struts atop the petals like
a showgirl. She hums a tune from her youth,
taps her fingers on the bed, hopes to grow eight legs.
But she is not ready yet, there is so much to do.

Her life is a shambles: who will sweep up the poems
scattered about like her grandchildren's
candies, or her children's homes?
Who will clear away the dishes left on the table
after Friday's dinner party, teach her seminar
next semester? And what will become of the faces
whose creases she has yet to record?

The window is locked, the curtains closed
but stars slide sideways through the glass,
whisper about the tunnel in the sky, streams
she will cross on the backs of serpents—a coming home
where she can slip off the layers of her skin.

"Not now!" she cries. "I have so many things to do."

In her next life, she fancies herself a waterfall
spilling over mountain cliffs, mighty and timeless,
splashing all who behold her: but not yet.
She turns her back to the window and her bones,
grown heavy with love, form their first cracks.

Listen with ears of tolerance!
See through the eyes of compassion!
Speak with the language of love.
—Rumi

Serendipity: A Golden Shovel

—after Adrienne Rich

Serendipity, I'll say, if you remember. My hands, slippery from
rainfall, fumbling for something in my bag that might startle you

as it crash-lands. Keys clattering onto pavement, a cliché I
play to keep the rain from sweeping you off the street. My want

of an umbrella, of shelter, of a steamy bubble bath, is more
metaphor than I care to reveal, but I want to leave no more than

I want to abandon my own chilled skin. In your hand, the keys I've
turned again and again, days clicking open, letting in the ever

present question of us. *Will we meet in the cheese aisle?* I've asked
myself, envisioning fondue and wine, tremble of candlelight, all

our fears melting in the soul of the moment. I'm thinking of
the song we would make our own, the sheer nakedness of it,

a ballad undressing itself lyric by lyric, its flesh reflected in the
mirror of our eyes. Mornings on the train, the newscasts'

headlines spun through the hands of a supersonic clock. Terrible
catastrophes are quaking our world, I want to say. Stories

of disasters, diseases, death. What, for God's sake, do you make of
the lesbian lovers in London, assaulted for not giving life

to a kiss? What sick deity cast us as porn stars, our love clad in
lingerie, or naked as rain sliding down a calla lily? I want my

thoughts to lift your chin without the benefit of voice. That time
I offered you a lozenge for your parched throat and you smiled the

smile of one whose body had forgotten: Prince on stage, knowing
what it means to kiss a woman, our skittish, haphazard hands, "it's

been fun" scribbled where I'd expected digits. The worse
for wear, I wandered the streets, more intoxicated from love than

beer, wishing for your name upon a cascade of starlight, that
the rock had sent me soaring into your aura and not the much-

rotted pile of litter, whose stench clung to my skin for days. Worse
is the jar I've kept like a keepsake, full of pennies, each coin the

face of an opportunity lost when words held their breath, knowing
serendipity might shun me and cease to cross our paths. What

do I know of love? Coffee in the corner of a café, the silence it
takes to will one's soul into the body of another. Love means

a jar of pennies, of which, all these years, no lover has managed to
guess their worth. If, now, you remember, I'll say I'd rather be

soaked to the bone than live uncertain whether serendipity lied.
You return my keys and I wait, raindrops splashing fro and to.

Messenger

Do you remember that day in December when you lost
your composure and flailed your arms against

the wind? I was sitting next to you in the snow,
writing another poem, curling letters into the shape

of something that would resemble love. When words
lost their footing down the slopes of my mind;

when I couldn't clear a tunnel through the avalanche
of emotions, I doodled hearts, roses, and rainbows

around the edges, interlaced with her initials,
reminiscent of the art we used to make for each other

in kindergarten. I could feel you breathing over my shoulder.
How childish you seemed to say, spraying my face

with frost. A sprinkle of leaves, laughter you couldn't stifle
or maybe you were proclaiming your treeness,

shedding the last of your foliage, a metaphor I was too young
to fathom. Unlike you, I was bundled up in red wool,

a splash of color on a dazzling white canvas—
I'm watching this, a shadow hand painting a picture

of a younger me onto my memory. Afraid to recognize
the coat, the snow, your bark wedged under my fingernails,

I rewrite myself in third person so that the girl could be
any girl, creasing pieces of notebook paper, binding them

as though strangling her poems. It's no use. My face
resurfaces again and again, like a body underwater.

The string, too, would tie my thoughts in knots,
would grow and twist and multiply into the rope

that tightened around the throat of my nightmares
until I startled awake, remembering. Gasping for air.

I like pretending she spotted me there tossing snowballs
at a tree. Longed for those whimsical girlhood battles

as much as I did. That she glided down the hill, all tinsel,
bells, and Christmas cheer, with some sparkling

trinket that represented remorse for three years of silence:
love, requited. Pretending myself into the body of the boys

whose lips warmed hers year after year, while I sit here
with your unwavering treeship around my shoulders

which should be enough but isn't. Some might call you
savage, but the blood you drew across her cheek as she ran

along the trail between her house and mine seemed at once
a miracle and a prophecy, the second chance that would change

everything. I should have helped her to her feet,
wordless. Applied snow to her wound, watched her flee—

I'm confessing now so you won't forsake me later.
If you don't kiss me again, I think I'll die, I said instead,

tucking my voice under my breath, hiding it even from you,
my lifelong confidante, who has watched me grow

like a flail of windblown branches, every which way
but out of my heart. Before we part; before I go away

for the last time, I offer you this sheaf of poems.
May you, on your journey, send my love homeward.

What I Left Behind

A playlist of songs we danced to in The Castro, first at the bar
where you undressed my barriers like bothersome lingerie.

Your painting of a moon goddess, my body gowned in streams
of light. The shaggy rug on which I posed nude, or nearly.

The set of keys you slipped into my pocket at Le Bistro D'Amour.
Un appartement à Montmartre? I fantasized in wretched French.

There was laughter once. There were days we doubled over with it
for no other reason than spilled coffee or a song sung off-key.

In winter, when the last embers had turned to ash,
the poems you breathed across my body to keep it burning.

The bedraggled kitten we found trembling in a bush. It was I
who carved her gravestone when she died, luxuriously, of old age.

The baby clothes we bought, washed, ironed, folded into drawers
then gave away. Blood on tile, the vestige of which never faded.

Later, a slew of socks tossed haphazardly around your bedroom,
the mismatched colors and patterns a testament to our relationship.

I don't mean the future I glimpsed through kaleidoscope eyes
in the days when any place was ideal for lovemaking

but whispered conversations wafting on air. I mean scraps of paper
with names and numbers. Unfamiliar scents, unfurled silence.

The dress I bought to match yours, stained red. The wine I spilled
when you got sloshed and called me by someone else's name.

Cheap souvenirs from faraway places, displayed on shelves.
The empty spaces, a map of lands we would never explore.

Poem of My Life

Driving back from the oncologist's office,
I stopped at a roadside diner
to write you the poem of my life.

I had intended to go straight home to you,
heat the good kettle to steaming.
I would have sat you down overlooking

the garden, the impossible bursts of color
we spent years cultivating, and broken
the news over iced lemon pound cake.

I had thought to reminisce about
the pride march that brought us together,
our raised fists captured in black and white

for posterity, the hum of the after-hours club
where we slow danced breast to breast
beneath dim, dust-filled lights,

knowing we could be raided and not caring:
everything that came after in your rented room,
so sparsely furnished it seemed naked.

What we found
and all that we lost along the way:
the loved ones who stopped loving us,

the lies we hissed through gritted teeth
in order to land jobs, or keep them.
The slurs spelled out in spray paint

on our front door, the stones that shattered
windows, the sticks that broke bones.
We weathered all the storms together,

got married in our sixties, our kiss captured
for posterity, this time in rainbow colors,
displayed like an Olympic gold medal

over social media. We had made a pact
to die of splendid old age in a single breath,
embraced on a bed of petals, and now this,

a fight we cannot win, no matter the strength
of love we brandish. So please forgive
my tardiness today, but I needed to set

these words to paper, let the ink weep
for a spell, before laying my head
in your lap to say goodbye.

Seagull

—for Belisa

Air was scarce but it didn't matter, my room a sudden rush
of family, nurses, patients congratulating the young woman
with new orange highlights, lipstick, glitter.
I told you: we're having a party today, honey.
This time they removed my colon, one less tumor

and more space inside for your stories, I said
as we skipped up and down the beach you had painted
in your four-year-old vision of things: the sun's flames
crackling in the corner, sea ripples more soothing than
morphine. Scattered seashells, birds dashing everywhere.

This is what I fought for, two years of your little-girl fingers
wrapped around mine, your laughter urgent, warming
as a waterfall spilled over my body, which I kept
rock-hard on the outside for your sake:
my muse, oblivious to your own magic.

One night, I couldn't open my eye, the lid
too weak to hold the tumor above. It was time
to step out of my body and take a flight to your
radiant beach, the home you had chosen for me.
At four, you taught me the insignificance of traitor

cells. You half-waved as I slipped out the window
and somewhere between cliff and sea I learned what birds do,
how the eagle cuts through the air like an elegant blade,
shimmer remaining long after its disappearing act.
But for you I became a seagull. I curled my claws

over the edge of the rock, unfurled my wings and swooped
onto the shore, where I collected the shells you wear
around your neck, wet and salty when you woke the next morning,
my final gift to you. When you think of me, listen closely:
you will hear my sea songs, remember my journey.

My Name Is Alma

I ache to describe the glass
from which our lives were cut.
So many líneas on my mother's face
I could never distinguish

a smile from a frown, but mostly,
her expression was a study in despair
and it took all my tenacity to keep from
cracking: the time an intruder held a gun

to our heads, stole every bare thread
of our piso. The time we pieced together
our meal from found scraps.
The gang that murdered my brother for

saying no, the note that said we were next.
Before our journey, she warned me about
sonido, how a whistle or hum could undo us
like a zipper pulled down on the shadows

we would wear at night. Los coyotes thought
nothing of pulling down zippers whenever
someone struck their fancy, even a schoolgirl
like me. Afterwards, my mother held me close,

soothed me with stories from her heart,
a balm smoothed over memory.
All those survival skills we had cultivated
in our old neighborhood sweltered in the sun

until they were reduced to drops, whether
sudor or lágrimas, it didn't matter: salt tastes
like salt wherever it may surface. Salt slapped
on a wound will make you think twice before

weeping. We had promised to protect
each other from thieves and thugs yet
our war cry amounted to a whimper of resignation
when they threatened to abandon us

to the mercy of that godforsaken desierto
among rattlesnakes and scorpions.
Whatever happens out here, she whispered,
you must shut the door on your mind

and keep walking. Even if your toenails
fall off. Even if a thousand shards of sky
come crashing down or the sand opens its
mouth, fangs glistening, and you're terrified

it will swallow you whole. Even if our fingers,
bound in the most intricate of nudos,
come untied and my voice is blown away
in a dust storm, keep walking.

Once you're on the other side, you'll be safe.
Safety meant a bedroom en la casa de papá
overlooking an exquisite garden. It meant
food to eat and books to read and streets

that didn't reach up to bite you.
Here, we are like insects squirming under
the glare of a microscope: googly-eyed,
limbs folded into unthinkable positions,

playthings of the guards. Hundreds
of bodies caked in dirt, blood, and snot.
Some are too frail to sit up; instead, they roll
from side to side, soiling the concrete floor

we sleep on. Mamá would be appalled:
at least we showered every day
back home. I've never been stuffed
in a hielera until now.

A baby pees into the void where a diaper
ought to be. How to say in English: a bullet
to the chest is preferable to death by humillación?
I wonder what has become of her.

Is she a fish floating in the Rio Grande,
all color and scales, or a jumble
of piel y huesos, heaped on an identical
concrete floor, reaching for me across cells?

Imagine

—after Gwendolyn Brooks

Dreaming, you said the hour was dry, our plans involuntary.
Imagine you were wrong. Imagine water, clear and fresh,

trickling into the sink where we wash our hands of the day's
dirt. Imagine our shoes gleaming, sleek as the coins

we relinquished to flee an afterlife looming over our shoulders
long before life had been lived. If our feet were free of the mud

we trudge through to pick carrots and tomatoes, perhaps we could
walk into a shop and buy a new shirt, a pair of slacks,

a solid hat to block the sun without leaving traces of our history
underfoot. Carrots and tomatoes for our own plates.

Look at our faces, caked with obscenities, spat at us from stuffed
mouths while the emptiness in our bellies inflates day after day,

balloons on the verge of bursting. I'm remembering the day
we released a bouquet into the sky and our daughter laughed

to think of heaven streaked in multicolor. In sleep her name
blurs on your tongue like a picture out of focus,

like a memory flickering on and off. Imagine our plan hadn't
failed and she were here on this pallet, lying between us.

I stroke your face, taut in sleep, trying to smooth the wrinkles
out of your dreams, wishing deference weren't a prerequisite

for survival, that we weren't herded into holes and shadows
at any threat of a raid, that our future weren't weighed

by the bucketful. That come sunup, we could lift
our heads, straighten our backs, stop imagining.

Left Behind

If it had all been a bad dream
and you had barreled through the front door,
ravenous after soccer practice,

homework sheets spilling out of your backpack,
you wouldn't have recognized me: eyes the shade
of storm clouds, a torrent caving my face.

I was proof that a man could grow as thin
as the streak that trails a bird in flight.
You would have said: *dad, why haven't you washed*

your shirt? There are ways to eradicate stains
but I wanted to wear your blood so that I might
collapse, intoxicated by your smell, stifle

the image of your body, motionless among the dead.
I fantasized about ghosts, how you'd animate our walls
with your shadow moves. How you'd raise the hairs

on the back of your mother's neck, as if pulling
one of your pranks, the kind that always got you
grounded but made us chuckle in private.

During the day we keep it together.
Nights, my mind shudders under the strike of memory.
You step onto the stage of my nightmares

dressed in blood, launch your spirit body into a leap,
my leap, the leap that didn't carry me far enough
to land in front of the shots. You leap in slow motion,

mocking my failed attempt at heroics. Reeling,
I roar into the void: *I never wanted to be a superhero!*
I only wanted to chest the bullets that cheated you

out of life. I came up short, son. For a time, I thought
we'd lost our only child, but that was before
I learned to see you in a gust of wind, tousling my hair.

Before I learned to trace your expressions in swirls
of sunrise. Before I learned to recognize your wave
in the wings of a butterfly, flitting among daisies

outside your bedroom. All those colors gathered
in your arms, I think you might splash them against
the window, startle me out of my stupor.

The Reasons I Won't Be Coming

are numerous, and I would hate to interrupt
such a beautiful rendition of "Wind Beneath My Wings,"

your fingers gliding over the keys like a falcon
in flight, my spirit billowing under your hands,

the notes rising and falling through the hall,
cascading, stormlike, over the mourners. So young

and you refuse to cry like the rest. When I could still
articulate my thoughts, I suggested the song

might be too advanced for you, but it was my favorite
and you spent your free time polishing the piece,

insisting that only in its true splendor would my voice
waft on the melody, drift into your ear like a secret—

we had always confided in each other, after all.
There were other signs you devised while I was dozing

which you noted down in flamboyant curlicues:
a picture toppling to the floor, a gum wrapper tossing about

in the still air, a faint kiss on the nape of your neck,
raising goosebumps. *Tricks you must learn*

once you've attained your celestial powers, you said.
I realized you had seen one too many episodes

of *Ghost Whisperer* but didn't say as much.
Outside, a flock of sparrows alighted on a branch,

shaking loose autumn leaves. I fell silent for a spell,
watching red and orange figures flutter toward the earth.

Soon, their skin would crack and scatter, leaving but a skeleton
of their former glory. You caught me in the mist of your eye

and I nodded, despite myself. I never believed in your
afterlife, your winding staircase scattered with lily petals,

your flossy angel's wings, even as I lay in my hospital bed,
eyes closed, furrowed body curling into its chrysalis

to await transformation, even as light poured into the container
my soul would soon relinquish. Now, I'd love nothing more

than to spread my wings, supple as a butterfly's, come to rest
on your shoulder, give you reason to say: *I told you so.*

Instead, I regard you from afar, from this inexplicable place,
the music wafting over me, your tears beginning to splash

onto the keys. After the grief, the rage, after the desolation
will come freedom. How could I, in death, ever deprive you

of life? As the last stark note skims across the silence
you look up, into the swell of faces, oblivious to my applause.

I study your visage, a lovelier copy of my own,
and I know you understand the reasons I won't be coming.

All that we are is the result
of what we have thought.
                —Buddha

The Places We Empty

There are so many things I could say right now.
The expletives would fly off my words if I opened my mouth,

released them. The daffodils know. Their colors have paled under
my glower. Their petals have curled and rocked like a child

crestfallen after a scolding. They cower as I approach with
pruning shears. It's not fair, but I need to clip something.

I could fill the sky with flocks of words, startling winged creatures
migrating from south to north, from the place in my stomach

where my anger has been nesting to the place on my face
where they would alight, flapping and squawking, in search of

sustenance. By sustenance I don't mean worms or fish.
It's blood I'm after. Words clash in mid-fight just as birds clash

in mid-flight, whirling around each other in a downward spiral.
I once saw two bald eagles, talons locked, descending through

a treetop. Only one flew away, a rabbit wedged in its beak.
I, too, could spread my wings, crash through our sliding glass

doors, into the kitchen where she's hacking vegetables for salad,
the knife landing within millimeters of her hand: a provocation.

I could give her the duel she desires. I could claw at her arguments
until they've become as maimed and bloody as a dying rabbit.

I could perch on the edge of my dignity, singing until she retreated.
In every burst of silence we die a thousand deaths. In silence

I hobble around our garden, searching for my voice among petals and leaves, for all my voices longing to echo across the sky.

Ice Rink

There's a morgue now
       where we used to go ice skating.
Wisps of silence, echoes catching their breath
       in the chilled air where pop music
used to bounce and zip above our heads.

But I can't tell you that.
       At five, death is a bug floating in a puddle,
a trace of sadness in your chest,
       fleeting as the ice that dusts your gloves
when you go sliding across the surface.

Death is a word you pull on and off at whim
       or fashion into a ball and toss at my face
to gauge my reaction. For science you draw
       a coronavirus with a smiley face.
I don't add the hands that strangle organs.

I can't tell you my nightmares:
       caskets wheeled through the entrance
along the same path you took your first wobbly
       steps on doll-sized skates, bundled in a ski suit,
helmet tilting off to one side.

Caskets clustered in the corner where I taught you
       how to fall. Shadows spinning out of control
in the place where you let go of my hands
       and glided all by yourself,
future ghosts wavering, unobserved, in your blades.

Caskets pressed shoulder-to-shoulder to make room
        for more, while outside, the living must remain
a cool meter apart.
        You wonder when you and your friend
will be able to stroke hand in hand again. I say:

let's pretend-skate around the living room.
        One day, when you land your first clean Axel,
how will I find the strength to cheer when all I see
        is a haze of bodies spilling out of caskets,
severed limbs skittering across the ice?

Funeral Toll

The doorbell doesn't ring, it tolls: once, twice.
This is when lights flicker, floorboards splinter
under my feet. When the door is not a door

but a portal to a ravaged world I no longer
recognize. I conjure up the courier holding three
packages from Amazon in his gloved hands.

He asks for my name, his voice hiding behind
a mask like a frightened child. But I'm the one
who's afraid of monsters: globular, spiked, deadly.

A gust of air swarms around me and I back away,
ask him to drop the boxes on my welcome mat,
unconcerned with breakage. Signatures have become

superfluous. My children, avid package openers,
fly toward me then freeze, caught in the warning
I spin in the space between us.

Don't touch the packages! a mantra in our home
as commonplace as *count to twenty when you wash
your hands.* In the kitchen, I've stashed

plastic gloves to open cardboard. I spritz
disinfectant, scrub the flesh off every item until
they are phantoms of their former selves.

This is when I peel off my gloves, touch
a corner I missed, brush an eyelash out of my eye.
One last toll and I see the graveyard, devoid

of mourners, no family or friends clad in black,
no heads bowed. Just a stranger, masked and gloved,
lowering my casket into the earth.

Again

—for Ahmaud Arbery

What good is poetry
when it can't bring the dead back to life?

There is no line of verse in this world
beautiful enough to lure the breath
out of a breathless mouth.

My words are not made of cloth
yet this poem is soaked in blood,

a four-hundred-year-old river running
red over America's fractured body
of which yours is but a drop.

What good is poetry when
shopping, reading, jogging,
et cetera while Black
warrants a bullet to the chest?

What matters about Black lives
is the ease with which names
are effaced, crammed side by side
in the bowels of indifference.

When I say may they smolder in hell,
I mean:
if only I could write the supremacy
off your murderers' faces, sandpaper it down
to a fine dust, asses to ashes,
the better to choke on, my fiends.

With a strike of my pen, I could knot
their sneers into a noose and lead them
to the nearest tree, but who gives a damn
about poetic justice
when they're bound to be cut free?

I could pray for you, Ahmaud,
drag my words across the page
like a funeral procession, but I wonder:

what good is poetry when all it can do
is kneel on a piece of paper and wail?

Wish

—for Ilene Misheloff

I wish I could recall the name of the movie
we saw together, a week before the earth
opened its mouth and swallowed you whole.

I wish I could remember if the popcorn we shared
was drizzled in butter or if we had popcorn
at all. Perhaps we opted for chocolate bars

since shells would have wedged themselves
under your braces and mine, speckling
our sprightly teen smiles. Yours was like

noontide sunshine spilling across creek bed stones,
across shadows cast by oak trees. I've often wondered
if you passed through the park, where your backpack

was found, unaware of the predator lurking
around the next bend, impatient to pounce,
or if you were lured into that elusive car

as you came strolling out of the alley,
thinking only of the ice your blade would cut,
of the air swirling around you as you catapulted

into a high-flying, body-blurring Axel.
It could have been any of us heading to the ice rink
for an afternoon lesson, our lives snatched

in a flash, a mass of dreams wrested from our chest.
If only I could see you again, I'd tell you I've never stopped
shuddering. I wish I could find the words to describe

the delight in your eyes when you pulled up
to my house and saw I was dressed in the same
gray pullover, the same pink and gray striped skirt,

twins for a day, we surely quipped, unaware
that your outfit would soon vanish without a trace
and mine would hang, lifeless, in my closet

for the remainder of the year. I like to think we saw
a comedy, that we howled at wisecracks, snorting
our soft drinks, that we whooped it up, raised a ruckus,

that you were extraordinarily happy. What I wish
for the person who stole you, should they ever
catch him, is better whispered in your ear.

Sometimes I behold your face in flowers or butterflies,
a spill of sunlight, the glint of a blade.
Always I wish for the miracle of your return.

Fly

—for Virginia

Persistent fly,
I follow your flight and I am spellbound,
reading stanzas in your patterns.
My words always seem half-stuck
in a bone, a nerve, an eyelid.

Why don't I smack you with a swatter?
Perhaps you are part spirit
blown along by a familiar breath.
As you swoop and dash about my face,
your wings glint iridescent, and I know you.

You flit from hand to cheek
humming a Brazilian lullaby.
I crumple more paper:
you have to learn how to dive into yourself,
you buzz.

You still know best the prints I leave
when I press my fingers on paper
to squeeze out an image.
I turn away: one teardrop
is enough to crush you.

On Our Way to School

They know nothing of time but the water it holds,
    the currents that carry them along like jellyfish,

their imaginations colored by any treasure
    that may surface in a puddle of sunlight.

Today was no different. On the path to school lay
    a rock, half-buried under a mound of earth, voice echoed

in memory, expression devoid of its former shine.
    They stopped and stooped, tangled up in curiosity,

ignoring my pleas to proceed. In another moment
    I might have shown them how to paint animals

on the face. I might have taken it home, slipped it under
    a microscope, marveled at the geometric shapes reflected

in their eyes. If you listen closely, you can hear
    the crash and splash of a million years inside

its belly, I might have said. But on a school morning
    a rock is just a rock: stony, cold, troublesome as death.

An obstacle best kicked to the other side of the road.
    We have no time! I shouted, a tsunami of threats

rising out of my mouth, looming over them
    as though my rage had brought forth the Kraken.

At last they sailed along the tide of time I clamor about
    every day, the kind that spins clocks, sweeps minutes

onto the forgotten shore behind us. The kind that
    blinded me to the sunlight trickling off their cheeks.

This Morning

A poem falls out of the sky veiled
in the fiery reds and oranges of dawn

as though some fanciful creature of my dreams
has set fire to my mind. Words have never flashed

so radiantly on a Sunday, in fact have never flickered
at all, and more than breakfast I crave the crackle

and burn in my belly, the ashes pressed into
my fingertips as evidence of an idea shaved to its core.

How splendid it would be to sit at my desk,
describe the images hanging across tree branches,

lying between blades of grass, hovering atop
a sparrow's wings. The entire piece blazes before

my eyes. Behind me, the apocalypse that threatens
to sweep across my imagination, char every word

in its path: sheets and blankets piled haphazardly
like wood, my bed roaring to be made.

My children giggling in their bedroom,
voices luminous enough to melt away the darkness

without resorting to the switch. They are famished,
fidgety, my wife is ironing, and the dishwasher

needs to be emptied. So many tasks to complete
before we venture into the glow of Valdenazar Forest

with friends. Outside, the sky has turned a cool gray
like rainwater or teardrops or irrevocable loss.

Coronaversary, April 12th, 2020

—for Olga

Feliz Aniversario, mi amor: the words I blow
across your pillow like fairy dust every year

to wake you. Today is different. A voice
unlike my own comes pounding across

my chest and asks: *how many people do you think
died yesterday?* Our silences fall across each other,

the moment pulled inside out when our children
crawl under the covers, giggling. They're too excited

about the Easter eggs hidden around our home
to notice the sorrow rumpled between us.

Last year, when your parents could cup
their faces without fear of contagion

and the metro air wasn't thick with spirits
of past riders, we indulged in lunch for two

in downtown Madrid, toasted to our marriage
above bustling streets, held hands, unaware

that skin fused in the ardor of an afternoon walk
would one day generate more than electricity.

Today we coax our children into the kitchen
with the promise of chocolate and cartoons.

We have two minutes and I want to enfold
our love in a metaphor, striking and timeless.

Instead, I clap for us, howl for our family.
I say: *we're lucky to be alive.*

Thanatophobia

*"What is life? It is the flash of a firefly
in the night. It is the breath of a buffalo
in the wintertime. It is the little shadow
which runs across the grass and loses
itself in the sunset."*
                    —Blackfoot Proverb

How many years will I rotate around the axis
of my own existence before I fold into myself,
before my life rolls to a standstill, like a child's ball
lost somewhere inside a thicket, deflated?

How many more wishes will I puff into the universe
on the backs of dandelion seeds?
There are times I feel like a butterfly, scales flaking
off my wings under time's ruthless thumb.

Imagine, they say: all your colors fertilizing the earth
so that future generations may flourish.
I don't want to embody that kind of beauty.
What good are colors without eyes to behold them?

When I think of my children, their kisses sagging
on my cheeks, sinking into the cavity my face
will become, their voices silenced as my mind
shuts down, my heart thrashes, trapped

like a wild animal inside my chest. The burning,
the shortness of breath. The fear. This must be
what dying is like. I never stepped in the lava
of my youth or held my breath in tunnels very long:

what if the mystical white glow is a hallucination
and there are no spirits wavering on the other side?
It's useless, really, this obsession for surmising
the circumstances of my own demise.

An owl could come crashing through my window,
scratch off my scalp as I'm composing this poem.
I could slip off a rocky mountain path, plunge
into the river below, be swept under the current.

I could be assaulted late at night as I toss
paper and plastic into their corresponding bins, drown
in a puddle of moonlight. Or none of this could happen.
Maybe at one hundred, I'll dramatize the most unremarkable

of denouements, slip into sleep, surrounded
by loved ones, my deathbed sprinkled with forget-me-nots.
A nice gesture, but it would be naïve of me to believe
that after I die, I won't forget or be forgotten.

In the meantime, how shall I rid my dreams
of the interminable darkness, the earth's steady rotation,
the years floating by in the millions like cosmic dust,
the crushing journey into the final void?

Notes

"California on Fire": The 2018 Camp Fire in California killed 85 people, mostly from Paradise. Then-President Trump blamed the fire on a lack of leaf-raking. "What She Remembers": I wrote this poem at the onset of the #MeToo movement, with Brock Turner heavy on my mind. "Ruled Suicide": In June 2020, 24-year-old Robert Fuller was found hanging from a tree in Palmdale, California, across from City Hall. Although his death was ultimately ruled a suicide, many still believe he was lynched. "Serendipity: A Golden Shovel": The end words form the first stanza of "To the Days," by Adrienne Rich, from *Dark Fields of the Republic* (W.W. Norton). In May 2019, a lesbian couple was harassed, assaulted, and robbed on a London bus after they refused to give in to the demands of four men who wanted to see them kiss. "Seagull": Belisa was a beloved cancer patient in Madrid. "My Name is Alma": In 2018, Donald Trump's administration enacted a cruel "zero-tolerance" policy for migrants crossing into the US. As a result, nearly 2,000 children were separated from their parents in April and May of that year. "Imagine": The first two lines paraphrase Gwendolyn Brooks's lines in "Kitchenette Building," from *A Street in Bronzeville* (Harper and Brothers). "Left Behind": I wrote this poem after learning about the 2019 El Paso, Texas Walmart shooting. "The Reasons I Won't Be Coming": "Wind Beneath My Wings" was made famous by Better Midler in 1988 when she recorded it for the soundtrack of *Beaches*. *Ghost Whisperer* was a television series starring Jennifer Love Hewitt, which ran on CBS from 2005 to 2010. "Ice Rink": In March 2020, as Coronavirus deaths began to skyrocket, Madrid's Palacio de Hielo was transformed into a makeshift morgue to help alleviate the pressure on hospitals and funeral parlors. "Again": In February 2020, Ahmaud Arbery, a 23-year-old unarmed Black man, was pursued by three white men and fatally shot while jogging. "Wish": On January 30th, 1989, 13-year-old Ilene Misheloff was abducted while walking home from Wells Middle School in Dublin, California. Her case has never been solved. The poems in this book are a work of the imagination.

About the Author

Julie Weiss received her bachelor's degree in English and Creative Writing from San Jose State University and moved to Spain the following year to teach English abroad. She found her way back to poetry in 2018 after slipping into a seventeen-year creative void. She was a finalist in *Alexandria Quarterly's* First Line Poetry Series and a finalist for *The Magnolia Review's* Ink Award. A Best of the Net Nominee, her work appears widely online and in print. Originally from Foster City, California, she lives in a former Spanish ghost town with her wife and two young children.

Kelsay Books
502 South 1040 East, A-119
American Fork, Utah, 84003

www.ingramcontent.com/pod-product-compliance
Lightning Source LLC
Chambersburg PA
CBHW022016080426
42733CB00007B/618